Every kid wants to be an all-star in something, especially in basketball!
But only the best can join the NBA.

I wanted to be with the all-stars, but I was small, and couldn't keep up with the big guys.
My father, who used to play with the stars, taught me how to shoot a hoop, but I thought I would never stand tall in the NBA.

My dad once told me to become an NBA player,
you have to be hungry for it.
I was starving! I wanted it like I wanted a burger.

I also tried other sports as well.
I played baseball, football, and soccer.
It's nice to try different things and discover
what you want to be, and I found my hunger
was still on basketball.

I decided to make basketball my goal.
I played in the sun, rain, and snow, feeding
my hunger for talent.

I learned how to shoot a mean free throw.
I became a pretty good player in a small
amount of time.

But I was still small. When you think of a basketball player, you think of someone who is tall enough to reach the clouds, yet I was under the other players like an umbrella.

My coach told me I was too small to succeed. I couldn't be a defender because I wasn't strong enough. It was enough to make most people quit.

But I didn't allow my small size to let me down.
I worked harder to prove that great skills can
come from small people.

After leaving high school, every college
told me I was too small and not tough
enough to play basketball.
Eventually, I did find a college that would
give me a chance: Davidson College.
It was a small college for someone small like me!

Everyone thought I couldn't do it. But I led the team to victory. I had the most points out of anyone, and I made our small college a big name as we became the final four in the tournament of the NCAA.
People started to talk about me.

Soon, the world didn't judge me by my size, but how I played.
I joined the NBA, playing for the Golden State Warriors.

My small size helped me win.
I was a point guard.
I threw the ball at the players who needed
it the most, and ran under the legs of my
big opponents with ease.

My team hadn't won a tournament in 40 years.
But in 2015, I helped my team to win our first
NBA championship in a long time.
I became MVP and wowed everyone who watched me.

My coach told me I shoot like someone guided
by a laser beam.
My laser beam is my hunger to be the best!

I may be small, but I'm always working to grow my skills! I hope to continue to lead my team to victory, and show the world not to judge a book by its cover.

To me, size doesn't matter.
But your hunger does.
How hungry are you to be the best?

Find something that fills you up, and be very hungry for it, eat it, and you will be the best at whatever you want to be!

Get more inspirational children books by Roy Brandon!

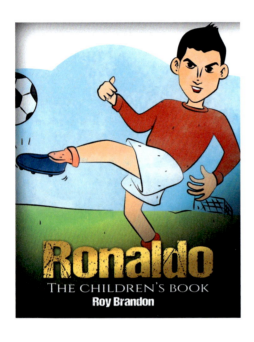

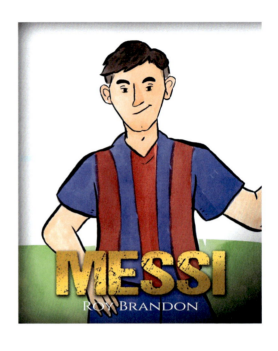

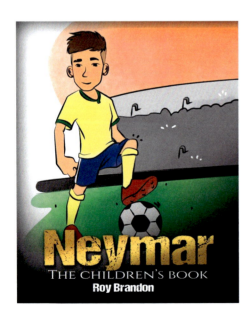

Visit www.RoyBrandon.com for more...

Made in the USA
San Bernardino, CA
31 May 2017